THIS BOOK BELONGS TO:

. . . .

. . . .

. . . .

. . . .

. . . .

. . . .

OTHER BOOKS YOU MAY LIKE

All Things Are Possible
Mark 9:23
(6 x 9)(Lined)
Blank Journal

https://www.amazon.com/dp/1721827323

I Can Do All Things Through
Christ Who Strengthens Me
Philippians 4:13
(6 x 9) (Lined)
Blank Journal

https://www.amazon.com/dp/1720298599

Hello,

Thank you for purchasing this book. We hope you have enjoyed using it as much as we enjoyed designing it. We are a small husband and wife business. Words cannot express how much we appreciate that you bought our book.

It would help us a lot if you could take a moment and leave a review about this book on Amazon.

Thanks again, Belle Journals

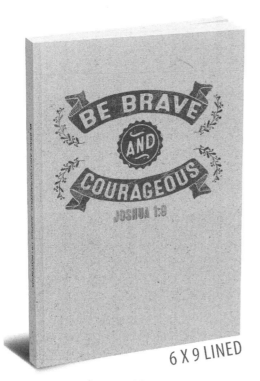

6 X 9 LINED

LEAVE A REVIEW
BUY IT AGAIN

Be Brave And Courageous
Joshua 1:9
(6 x 9) (Lined)
Blank Journal

https://www.amazon.com/dp/1721989013